ANOTHER CITY

ANOTHER CITY

POEMS

David Keplinger

MILKWEED EDITIONS

Published 2018 by Milkweed Editions

Printed in the United States of America

Cover design by adam b. bohannon

Cover photo by Eugenio Marongiu

Author photo by Czarina Divinagracia

18 19 20 21 22 5 4 3 2 1

FIRST EDITION

Milkweed Editions, an independent nonprofit publisher, gratefully acknowledges sustaining support from the Jerome Foundation; the Lindquist & Vennum Foundation; the McKnight Foundation; the National Endowment for the Arts; the Target Foundation; and other generous contributions from foundations, corporations, and individuals. Also, this activity is made possible by the voters of Minnesota through a Minnesota State Arts Board Operating Support grant, thanks to a legislative appropriation from the arts and cultural heritage fund, and a grant from Wells Fargo. For a full listing of Milkweed Editions supporters, please visit milkweed.org.

LIBRARY OF CONGRESS CATALOGING-IN-PUBLICATION DATA

Names: Keplinger, David, 1968- author.

Title: Another city : poems / David Keplinger.

Description: First edition. | Minneapolis, Minnesota : Milkweed Editions, 2018.

Identifiers: LCCN 2017050712 | ISBN 9781571314864 (pbk. : alk. paper)

Classification: LCC PS3561.E5572 A6 2018 | DDC 811/.54--dc23

LC record available at https://lccn.loc.gov/2017050712

Milkweed Editions is committed to ecological stewardship. We strive to align our book production practices with this principle, and to reduce the impact of our operations in the environment. We are a member of the Green Press Initiative, a nonprofit coalition of publishers, manufacturers, and authors working to protect the world's endangered forests and conserve natural resources. *Another City* was printed on acid-free 100% postconsumer-waste paper by Thomson-Shore.

For Kermit Moyer
A willingness of the heart

CONTENTS

CITY OF BIRTH

One lives so badly, because one always comes into the present unfinished, unable, distracted. I cannot think back on any time of my life without such reproaches and worse. I believe that the only time I lived without loss were the ten days after Ruth's birth, when I found reality as inde-scribable, down to its smallest details, as it surely always is.

RILKE TO HIS WIFE, CLARA: PARIS, SEPTEMBER 13, 1907

The City of Birth

The wound rips open: You feel the welt
of solitude, its hospital lights. Then you know
you have arrived. It is to be one body
and held in the palm of the doctor's hand.
It is the gash of being seen.

Now for the rest of your life
you are trying to be born through a wound.
That's loneliness. By a slip, or by some move
more desperate, you have burned
a purple shadow on your body.

But death is not the subject of our portrait.
It is the knowing you are seen,
it is the lighting of one's light, it is to take
a body, knowing you are not the body.
That's loneliness.

Ardor

My place was under the table.
I remained there like a muffled lamp.
Seated above me, along my table-sky,
my parents and their good friends
laughed so hard my planet shook.

They struck their matches, tiny plosives.
Against the table-sky they slammed
their fists. One man was very drunk.
He fell down like he had been pushed.
His eyes met mine at my place under the table.

My small green soldiers, too,
would sometimes lose their dignity.
It was the quality I loved about them.
They all had in common an absolute
sureness, their ardor to die.

Preservation

The Little Boy Blue on the wall at ease
in his leggings, hips sashayed. The Pink Girl
shadowed by her measly parasol. The figures
never aging, man on his horse, her pearl
jawline round and bursting with a toothache,
in agony, her horse eyes, their logic
human, looking at my looking back at you.
Because I was the only one left in the room.
Because I will be always. Because I will be
always. Because you suddenly let go of time.

The Brahms

After the words of Leon Fleisher,
a concert pianist who suffered forty years
of focal dystonia in his right hand

Those years I thought of little but the Brahms.
The left hand grew bored. Play Brahms, I told the right.

But the hand hit the keys like a fist. The Brahms
would travel from my brain along the right

of my shoulder and then from triceps into bone,
where it would die—or almost die—all right,

or it hung like a fish in cold shallows, the Brahms
suspended, not dead. Then my constant urge to right

the thing or force it down my arm. "To play the Brahms,"
my teacher scolded, "you have to listen," and he was right,

first to listen to the quarter notes as they began
like breaths. First to hear the language of my rite:

Brahms, play. Play the fingers of the hands, Brahms,
make me your instrument, your left hand, your right.

Beatification

And yet I honored thee—as the wise will deem—rightly.

ANTIGONE'S FINAL SPEECH

The only soul   who beatifies itself
is the lightning bug   of America

also called Firefly   also called
Half-in-love-   with-dusty-death

also called   Slant-of-light
also known as   Hobo-who-believes-

he's-Jesus   and You-
oh-my-soul   greased with luciferase

my consort   arriving on fire
as *Lampyridae*   your flash dactylic

like apple tree— crucifix—
undertow—   you are the one

lit from inside   as you venerate your life
to children   and I chased you   a long time

through darkness   my hands
thrust forward   when I sealed shut my fist

like a cave door   and squeezed—

Embarrassment

En route to California, after crossing snowy Monarch Pass, I'd pull into a bar on Highway 50 called the Bear Claw. At his table my dead father sat in the green sleeveless jacket with orange on the inside. Or now and then the jacket was reversed, depending on whether he was hunting me or hiding.

Where have you been, I asked him, and he told me of the cities he had visited in death: Cherbourg, France, where there was a disappointing fistfight, and the streets of Manila, where he thought his murderer had been following him, but it was only himself as a young man, holding a pair of lost glasses in hand. In Port-au-Prince he had been a child living off crisp fish he ate in tiny bites, cooked over a barrel by the sea. He had been in my mother's house many times, unable to fix his contraptions as one by one they failed her.

My father was a man always crouched in a pose against embarrassment, which I inherited. So I understood. That's why I never reached California, and I would turn around each time, risking my life all over again on Monarch Pass.

Lovesickness

Here's how it is
with the lovesick.
One octopus loved
her naturalist
until the giant, ink-
filled head remained
permanently settled
on her shoulders,
looking upward
from the aquarium
as the other gazed
down into it. Then
an egg the size
of a grain of rice
fell from the octopus.
Distance is sometimes
confused for love.
I've begun to feel so far from myself,
I want to have a child.

Citizen Thumb

Oh my thumb, my damned thumb,
I've stuck you with a hook.
I've fattened you with hammers,
frozen you in winter lakes, tanned you
like the faces from the peat bog.

At the lunch meat counter, once,
you cheated on the scale, and then I
punished you, exiled you, antagonist,
opposable, assigned you no number,
neither zero nor one.

I've killed you many times.
Each time, I felt your weight, a pietà.
Each time, I resurrected you.
I jammed you all my childhood
into the hot tomb of my mouth.

Citizen Small

For a long time the small of my back
was stable and I could fall down

when surprised and make everyone laugh,
especially my wife who shocked me

more and more, merely to seek the effect,
the disappointment splitting open my face

and then the buckling of my legs as I
seemed to fold forward and backward

at once like an origami lotus. But after a while
the fall began to cost me hours, days, feeling

the sadness in the small, as if it were a city
of disgruntled people who happened to occupy

the seat of a country no longer young
and which should know better. Nevertheless

I kept falling for anyone who asked me to,
buckling under myself until it was harder

and harder to get up, until I remained hunched
down long after everyone had left the room

and I was alone with the small, in the country of my injuries.

My Father's Hours

I went searching for a clue
of some collaboration

between the two
who ruled that house

with its discouragements
for a glance or the Morse

of clicking silverware
as on the late-shift nights

over the chair he hung
his heavy green coat

and then his hard hat
by its strap of white plastic

and like a man
in an elevator falling

he would stand frozen
the work still loud in his body

What was the story he told himself
coming home on these evenings

was his life

when I met him at the door

in my pajamas of men on motorcycles

all of them helmeted impassive

doing wheelies in the air

Now up the wooden hill he said

and he pointed his finger

at nothing

Citizen Mouth

I eat a ripe tomato this way: I bite into its face
like a softening pear, leave behind a maw.
And the onion skin, my book of Revelations,

I chop with my teeth down to proverb size.
On the cutting board an apple, stripped and wet, lights up
the room. I like my lard and swallow it, it

passeth through the teeth and the cave door of the throat,
passeth the uvula's cobra head. I eat and I do not resist.
Whatsoever I eat is my Lord and God, my honored guest.

Citizen Eye

I'm sent back into bed,
that's how it was.

Muscular and tense,
my father paces

with a jaw-like wrench,
our pipes about to blow.

My mother lies
on her side of the room.

Even in the dark
I see the faces on my coins

spread across the bureau.
All the eyes are open.

City of Youth

Gray ocean wedging
under your gray feet,
and I am looking at you

when you were still a brazen girl,
ten years before
my birth. A day

at the Steel Pier.
The photograph
scalloped into a square,

white border, dated
June 1957. For sixty years
there is your towel,

there is the trash can
you pose in front of,
there is your sandy

left thigh. There is your face:
outlined by makeup: sixty
years ago. Always

it is possible
to mark in your gaze
something else; that is,

how it grows suspicious
of the photographer,
or of the ocean behind him;

or to say you are squinting
because the sun
must be rising

over the Atlantic
and the Steeplechase sign
and the east;

and to see something
else: your rented,
striped umbrella;

and something else: a woman
behind you, running,
who is blurred now

into a turreted cloud,
no face at all, already on her way
to something else.

Broadcast for the Last Snowfall

It's nearly gone, but the sky
is white filings a few more moments, and the land
is a magnet. It was once very cold
on my planet, we want to confess

on radio waves shot past the sun,
it was all like the cover of the *Saturday
Evening Post*, or a December
in the Poconos, the shuttered store

with a couple of manikins watching
from otherwise empty windows, in summer wear.
It's almost here, while the sky breaks
loosely, when all this snow will be drunk

up by the oceans again: and the oceans,
too, will be dry by sunset, as the witnesses
just stand there in their sunglasses,
like we do now, looking out and laughing at something and pointing.

Lazarus

I'd cut my hand wide open in the middle
of the night. So the ER doc described,
to calm me down, how one time she had saved
a severed thumb, brought in swaddled in a towel.
I have been thinking ever since, now that I'm sober,
how the thumb woke up as if nothing at all
had happened, pale Lazarus bent over
and brought to full height. How the severed part would heal;
how the color would come back; but also how
the thumb would have been, like Lazarus, always a little
numbed after that, always off kilter a little.
The doc explained this—part in disgust, now
I realize—as she sewed the wound into a curse.
It still feels drunk, the way I move my fingers.

"Every Angel Is Terrifying"

After a translation of Rilke by Stephen Mitchell

There was the time   one of the younger deer
stepped into the hedges at the house
that we called Homewood   and through an open window
he lowered the shale-colored muscular shoulders
his eyes met my eyes   and pushed   partway through

I thought it was to see who was alive in here
or to offer some encouragement   with his aware
impassive face   may I stay heavy on this mind
I found myself requesting   may part of me remain
behind these eyes   but it did not   the herd continued

down their unmown road and the deer   at the window
broke his gaze and turned   and followed them
This was the start of some new work for me
it was the fall
I had been trying to untangle all my questions   I wished

that I was not myself   I never saw the angel after that
time passed   nor did the herd return
I went back to what I had been doing all along
except that I could feel   a certain focus   the concentration
of a being   standing watching   what I am

Mynah Bird, Hobe Sound

To come from far off. Feathers, cellophane,
shine over a gone-beige dish. Nothing to eat
but the dirt and old nails. The beak, perched

at the end of the nose, is the helicopter leaf
I recognize from childhood. So the mangroves sway.
I love the mutilated wreckage of it:

the way she folds one wing above her head
at the puddling fountain—lurching like the burglar
avoids the camera's aim. So many dinosaur years

on earth, playing along to the tree voices.
To come by oneself. To be gregarious, invasive.
The ears keep hearing new ways she can sing.

Magnification

I was not one of them. But I watched the users use.
Chantelle used only when she waitressed, part of her
self by the ice machine, smoking a cigarette,
while another part was bending over a stranger,

flattening a tablecloth, setting down a plate of
bronzed veal. Charlie the bartender drank no alcohol. He used
through the eye, and at forty the eye was terrible.
It is a city I remember only at night. I kept waking

up while the chefs chopped fish bodies into neat,
unnaturally square portions. And the kitchen smell
of yesterday's mashed food, sprayed clean from the sinks.
The ghost in the walk-in, telling me he's cold.

Charlie the bartender, already there when I arrived.
I watched him touch the needle to his blinking face.
He'd brace the eye with two fingers: a jeweler's glass.
Nothing was itself alone. In this way, it all grew larger.

Three

After I called the undertaker
and his son, I sat with the
corpse of my father; I told my father,

Smooth sailing now; I placed
the lock of hair into its envelope;
then I let these men come in.

The men would leave no mark.
They would not remove
their overcoats. They wiped each

shoe three times at the door,
the envelope still unaddressed
where it lay flattened on the table.

They stood above my father,
his new tattoos, his unflexed
relaxed face, and the robin's egg

shine of his fingers. Then I had to
please step clear? I did, and on three
they heaved the sheeted body.

Calling Horses

La Junta

She calls our horses back through dark,
calls out of trees and land the running horses,
calls horses wild with their own thinking,
corral a cloud of dirt and tantrum kick.

It is her angriest voice, the hardness
like the voices of the gods through canyons.
It is knowing what is sent will be returned.
It is this voice in her I've never understood,
but horses do as she expects of them, they come

to her loud clapping. They come because she asks.
She calls our horses back through dark
until the last, the penitent, who bends
so she can run the metal comb along the belly,
clear out the froth of white, protective sweat.

"An Apartment in the City of Death"

After a line by Kabir, translated by Robert Bly

When I died
I moved into this empty

room. I thought
about who stayed here

before me: their hard
faces from the nineteenth

century, the wan
cheekbones, the true

God they believed, the
body a

lackluster horse.
Not so much as

a single white candlestick
remains of them.

Not a flayed broom,
not one matchbook, not

a wood umbrella
camouflaged in shadow.

Soon, like they did,
I'll have stayed on so long

I'll be forced to die
all over

again. Then I'll huff off
to another city, smaller

room, away from here.

CITY OF TEXTS

Part of the terror is to take back our own listening.

HILDEGARD VON BINGEN

Wave

Lincoln, leaving Springfield, 1861,
boards a train with a salute: but it is weak.
To correct it, he slides his hand away
from his face as if waving, as if brushing
the snows of childhood from his eyes.

The train is moving east.
In the window Lincoln watches his face.
You'll grow old the moment you arrive,
he says to this face, which says the same to him.
But you will never reach great age.

The train speeds like a cortical pressure wave
in the left lateral sinus, say, a bullet in the skull.
Then he will have his salute. Then they will love him.
Then eternity will slow, fall like snow. Then the treaty with huge silence
which he, his face exhausted, must sign.

Arrival of the Aleph

Come May the buttercups
were smashed by the rains. And me:
I hung drenched with no coat on the Paratrooper ride.

Alone like a spider dangling
I watched from my tree in heaven
as the carnies, drunk, swung on their enormous levers

and huddled in impromptu shelters
like Phoenicians weathering a gale.
They had traveled from the ancient world to get here. And me:

I was already starting to feel
the swell of my tonsils. I was going to have to suffer.
I was going to hear the doctor demand—until I gagged—*say AH*.

Three Feasts: Simone Weil

Your mother stands by the stove, her feet spread too wide, pre-
paring like a weight lifter to heave two hundred kilos over her
head. Inside the oven is the roast. Your mother bears the meat
out of the oven, lifting it into the air like an Olympian. The
mother with her fireproof gloves waiting. The father puffing
exclamations with his pipe. But you will not eat.

* * *

In the three weeks at the camp in Casablanca you are starving at
some small café, never snapping for a waiter. It is 1942. To eat
is to sing in a slaughterhouse at the top of one's lungs; to eat is
to deny the ugliness, and you must watch the feast from outside.
Abide. Casablanca is a haven full of the astral ghosts, men in
dinner coats, the hunger for transfer papers. The young priest
at the church takes in the blessing—lit in agony—and even he is
eating God.

* * *

But could you taste this morsel? the small nurse asks you at the
end. Could you have water? The room is bright white air, fat-
tening and sudsy as the foam of beer. In Ashford they do not
know of you, what you'd become, your sense of ugliness and its
strange corona of light. Could you be one of us? Would you
taste of this? But you would not. Merely breathing was a kind of
wanting to belong.

The Crow's Progress

The crow took up its work inside the belly
of a struck-dead deer, dragged to the side of the road.

It began as subtle movement
from within the body,

then I imagined it, huge heart of a dinosaur,
angle of its shoulders, the sloppy wings,

slathered in the fluids of the deer's collapse.
It made the chest pound again. It made

the belly ripple. It was trying to be born.
By a mounte on the morne meryly he rydes

it was said of Gawain, on a deadly road,
no luggage but the joy of his own trouble.

The crow, too, was making soft and steady progress.
It scraped and scraped outward with its shovellike beak.

Night of the Death of Seeger

Trades Union Hall, Melbourne

As blows the cloods heelster gowdie ow'r the bay,
we sing, so like the infant's sounds,
who tries to sing with us. He sits and mouths
atop his mother's skirt and she sings to the boy,
his father drunk, the "Freedom Come All Ye,"

the man's song only spit and ululation.
As blows the cloods heelster gowdie ow'r the bay,
she sings, about bad weather, one bad season,
and the little baby, small Osiris,
rides in the canoe the skirt makes of her thighs,

As blows the cloods heelster gowdie ow'r the bay,
where he floats through the world's great glen,
not knowing his own life, aware of no crisis,
his song the gurgle sound of G—G—G,
first sound on earth, all spit and ululation.

Lightest of Dogs, Rome

Bowlegged, head bowed,
lightest of dogs, whose
bones show through,

I have nothing, no matter
how hard you study my hands.
Up on their balustrade

the aging waiters gather
to eat. Their voices riffle
over the bread and the wine.

But you have decided
to give this a rest. And you
lie down, and sigh through

the snout for a world
that has ended, the teacher
of Old Latin grammar.

Her Sums

Our teacher draws a giant *0*, a cipher.
"What's the distance from zero to one?"
The quiet girl, June Anne, won't answer
when she's summoned to the board.

Her father, this winter, fell looped
to his horse: was dragged by the force
of its physics. But it is spring and June
Anne is back at the board,

back at her terrible penmanship,
her timid voice, and she does not know
the answer, which I know is infinite.
It is infinite! I scream it in my thinking voice.

The question is hard, but it's easy.
It does what everything here does.
It makes you shut your eyes. It dizzies
by its science—drags you upside down.

Q: In What City Does Your Mother Live

In which she wears the jeweled shell
sometimes called the scarab beetle
who colors its walled castle bloody.
She wears the scarab Monday
when she drinks back fat white pills.
She wears it Tuesday when she falls.
She wears the scarab Wednesday
with the shredded lips that pray
to only swallow, turning blue. Thursday
with the angry morphine. She will try
to talk again on Friday, not to be asleep.
Saturday they wash with oil and soap.
For all that, Sunday is the law. Sunday
in her castle, folded wings and walls.

The Liquid R

It was a language of white hills, red brick towns.
    An alley was a comma in the agony's grammar.

It was the old one tied against a chair, madness
    swelling like a thought too big for her head,

and each death was a period. The mortician a stain,
    a drop of ink in his black suit, before a page-white mausoleum.

It was a language of yeast soup, snowy hills, towns
    called Beauty and Cold, where the names of things

had some corresponding order, beauty always going
    cold, always losing itself to something permanent.

There was carp at the fishmonger, butcher paper
    where the meat was weighed. Time at the clockmaker's shop.

There were syntactical surprises: the headmaster
    turned janitor inside of a day, the ambassador

seen on the subway in tattered clothes, the president
    dressed as prisoner, delivering his acceptance speech,

the secret police as tourists on their own beat.
    But mostly it was a language one used when speaking

in a whisper, rolling the *R*, practicing the *R*
   in your mouth until it dropped from the palate

to the tongue as from the pocket of God, and hung there
   momentarily in its shiny majesty, a sound much older

than the language that spent it, that offered it from one mouth
   to another.

Chance

On the train to Copenhagen I see Christina again. It's still the 1980s. I'm still a student of logistics with my backpack full of texts. Christina's hoping she will find some work at the casinos. One summer in the white apartment in Copenhagen, I shared a bed with her and her lover, Jens. I'd pretend to sleep while they fucked quietly. We would all lie in the bed the next day smoking King cigarettes. I am holding a cigarette and Christina is holding a cigarette. It's the moment chance has clasped into a quick and easy knot. We see in the other what it would have been like. To meet her like this: not *what* but *how* were the chances; how blurrily they course like trees; and at the doors of our separate compartments we are sliding shut the locks. It's still the 1980s. I'm still so good, I'm still stupid with my long hair and embarrassing excuses. I have a narrow bunk that pulls out like a drawer.

Tennis with the Dead

I'm playing tennis with the dead
and it's my turn to serve.
My partner is a friend of mine
from childhood, bouncing, lithe
again in his body, who died
in a bike crash. We're up against
two Aztec sacrifices. It is Quetzalcoatl
who sits in the referee's chair
atop his too steep pyramid.
My friend bends at the waist
and waits for me. There is a heart
in my hand, which I hurl in the air.

The Sibilant

We had the Latin of the waves at night.
We had the vernacular of tears.
We had the alternate ending, plan B,
in which we stayed together. We had
plan A, in which we would part.

We had the letters I have burned,
in which you spoke of our past life
as married, in a forest, on bicycles,
the trees angry seraphim, and darkness
coming. We had this now, not that.

We had that once, now this.
The sun was neither rising nor setting.
Our kisses plosives. The sex, the one time,
is sibilant: *shh*, before you cross the room
in a nightgown, the knock at the door.

Carp

Because it has fed
on the bottoms of rivers, and got fat,
we buy the carp at Christmastime.
It bends in its U in the porcelain tub.

With rolled-up sleeves my father
lifts the carp, winds a white rag
round its eyes. He uses the hammer
to quiet the suck of its mouth,
the tail's denials, its thumping.

The carp was introduced in Western water
seven hundred years ago. But it came
from farther east: its body continually
revising itself. He opens it with one slice
down the side, his awful Bible.

A Young Man's Copybook: 1861–1864

After the journal of my great-great-grandfather, Isaac P. Anderson,

who fought for the Union 88th Pennsylvania Volunteers, later incarcerated

for desertion after his discharge papers were stolen by a claims agent

CONSCRIPTION, SEPTEMBER 1861

By train we come to Philadelphia,
conductors patrolling

for drunkenness, illness, the mad.
We are no drunks. We are not ill.

We believe with our right minds, we say.
Come, they say, and we are greeted by steam, horse breath,

curt personnel, small cards that bear the family name.
From as far as Chester County, to the fortresses

of Quaker villages, we come to affix
to the rest of our days this

service: submission
to rank, by signature.

*

When we were little children, we would write
as children do, with pencil tips. We wrote

our stories in great loops, each practiced letter
scaled to the size of the thumb.

From my shoulder Jacob read out words
and I pressed down the words. The words

were my pressed flowers, the words
would flatten as flowers do. The pencil left

light markings, easily erased, like everything
I touched back then. I did no harm

with words. But outstretched like a stinger
in my father's fist would be the Cornwall pen:

that was my first weapon,
unalterable its strokes.

*

Where is he now, my Jacob
who pressed flowers in the pages of my copybook,

whom I reproached for being delicate.
Where am I now, who drew broad signs, flags, eagles

toting banners in their grip.
Where is the train that rocked me out of sleep

and Jacob at the window, hollering.
The sun almost up. Philadelphia: a field of smoke,

horse breath, curt
personnel, their tents and protestant, plain desks.

I have never seen the young more joyous in the world,
dressed that morning by our mothers.

*

A SKIRMISH BETWEEN WARRENTON AND
THE RAPPAHANNOCK, AUGUST 24, 1862

Already sick with what got in my lung,
the hot, then cold, then sweat

along my dewy spine,
through the left kidney, boiling, freezing,

then they came, hoots like geese from far away,
the small explosions, their light in darkness.

August, in the flanking march, I don't remember
but a man whose face was flush

against the magic flash of cannons.
His cap fell to the left. He reached to touch the cap.

I drove the bayonet into his left: his left:
as through the air, the clouds, my blood,

the sea of murky germs that multiply
in heat. Then, I swallowed him.

*

THE DEAD ON CULPEPER ROAD

It had become the natural thing.
Dead animal smell.

A long line of parade watchers, faces
turned toward the light rain.

I will never go back to Culpeper Road.
The gourd of a pumpkin

reminds me of a man's head
stabbed into a fence post.

Twelve nights on Culpeper Road.
The world a pit of parades and disuse.

Culpeper Road, if you come for me,
I will not go along, sir. I left.

The morning rose like a curtain, sir.
I was the hero. This was my play.

Crows were quacking like ducks.
Ducks were taking easy flight.

Guns were being fired far off, no louder
than a hoofbeat.

*

WHEN WALT WHITMAN CAME

TO STONE GENERAL HOSPITAL, APRIL 1864

We mewled to him
　　More peaches
and a bowl of cream

and called him Father
　　Walt, and he then gave
a nickel when he had

a nickel, and he then fed
　　a strawberry, its hairs
like the tongue of a cat

on my tongue
　　on days I would ask,
Did you bring me

the *Iliad*? And Walt sang,
　　Rage be now your song
in a voice that caught

and flung against the high–
　　ceilinged warehouse
and its walls, falsetto

unlike the sergeant
    but as detached as news.
The wheels of carriages

outside bore mounds of us
    away, arms, legs, hands,
more parts of us cut out

into something heavy
    for the long straight
roads where they would burn.

Walt Whitman's
    voice was curvy,
full of ruts.

He kissed us on the
    forehead, then on the lips,
then on the cheek.

*

MUSTERING OUT

I walked that wet
road home. It was

my birthday. I saw
a street, another street,

a series of houses
that led to my house,

its tiny door, I took
the door, I sat at a

table, small folded
napkins, a miniscule

world I could not
touch, set with Sevres china.

*

AFTER CHARGES OF DESERTION, JUNE 1864

I saw my river, one kid

stood fishing there,
not even waving

to a passing man
in uniform. My long

coat brushed
the ground, I was taller,

in my boots,
maybe my feet

weren't touching, my beard
the only weight,

like leader fishing line,
my hair like tippet,

and that's
my story, that's when

the cough discharged,
the sad, black

blood—exit ink.

*

On record I'm a cad, the object of a bounty, rogue escaper from
the rough.

My lawyer like a doting mamma walked to and fro with his black
bags, between the offices on Small Street.

But the word had dried already.
Think of my face:

A face the witness reconstructs.
A face that takes its leave.

V-Sign

The shape of birds
   like an open scissor
      against a length of cloth.
         It is gray cloth today,

as the sky is often gray
   in rural Pennsylvania.
      The scissor lays its V
         across the sky unfaltering,

an expert seamstress
   like my Aunt Sarah,
      who worked at the hosiery
         on Herbert Street.

She darned the ends
   of stockings for women,
      the flattened legs stretched out
         on the table,

and when the whistle blew,
   she just left them
      where they lay, all night,
         in the shape of a V.

X, & Axe

The world in which we live is not the only one in which we shall live or have lived.

FROM GÖDEL'S PROOF, 1970

From down this creek
    came men on flatbeds riding
on the wide green world
    as it was then.

There was a team of nodding
    broken horses,
there was a team
    of men I never saw before

who broke the old barn
    into its packet-parts,
board and beam and windowpane,
    hutch and doorframe,

who flattened down
    the imperfections
to a chart of transits,
    an equation for which x

would be the labor of their hands.
    Then rode backward
on the flatbed facing
    where the barn was razed:

our hands raised waving
       as they left. They have gone
on forty years, riding
       backward on the flatbed

the barn gone too
       the meadow gone
all gone downcreek
       although I cannot say

how it was they took it
       with them, made it small enough
to carry through the slit
       of twilight,

as through the two bars
       of an equals sign they disappeared
between the darkness
       and the land.

"Marie Curie's Century-Old Radioactive Notebook Still Requires Lead Box"

A book that casts its own light
and a hundred years since you,
who lived a spell in the tick
of its lamp, stood from your chair.

The book is closed and finished,
but the box must be lit from inside,
so I can see you thumb another
page, each new page brightening.

If I mentally turn on the lamp,
if I were to open the lead-vested
box: maybe I would find you there,
your gaze like a photograph seared

into the page. You finished this book.
You will not return to it. Also
you must stay here, obsession being
what scorches but does not burn out.

The Little Stairs of Z

The puffs of rising Zzs above my head,
I'm about to fall asleep, to climb
them well beyond the borders
of my cartoon cloud, when I hear
the first horse huff and stamp its foot.

It is the palomino, Sailor Boy,
dead for twenty years. Then not only horses
but the snails I met in Assisi, so small they climb
the blades of grass. Then the boxer
I carried up steps all her life,

the front right leg never healing.
What is the sun you've made of yourself
she asks, and all the animals stand waiting.
With the rile of the calves brought to the slaughterhouses
of my childhood. With the monkeyish cat, leukocytes
amok like mice.

Comet

Lincoln, returning to Springfield
in his coffin, the third of May, fell victim
to imperfect embalming, so, nearly
three weeks passing, his face took on
a fast collapsing, melted gaze.

If there were some way
he could see what he'd become,
grotesque, green Jesus of the hour,
returning dead to the dead he left here,
including one son, he would have turned his head.

He would have signaled
for the train to keep traveling.
He would have let the towns blaze past him,
the cities of the living, people pointing
with their hands, his death a tail of ice.

CITY OF DOMES

His mother called them his gems and often asked him why he liked things that were worn and old. It would have been hard to tell her. But there was something about the way in which the link of a chain was worn or the thread on a bolt or a castor-wheel that gave him a vague feeling of pain when he ran his fingers over them. They were like worn shoe-soles or very thin dimes. You never saw them wear, you only knew they were worn, obscurely aching.

HENRY ROTH, *Call It Sleep*

My Carnation

In the city I'm traveling to,
awnings billow up in wind and light.
Winter is early. We are surprised
we are surprised. The waiters
in their tiny jackets pull their jackets

close against the sudden cold.
In the city I'm traveling to, I arrive
on the train, its only passenger.
A man in black clothes helps me down.
A constable is twirling his baton.

A servant bears my latched-up trunk,
but ruefully, ruefully. He is gone.
A certain old woman is waiting to sell me
my carnation: to offer it with one hand,
to cover her teeth with the other.

An Ashtray

Once it sat at my grandfather's table
while he ate. Once it waited near the hot
cream faucet in his barbershop. Few smoke
like that anymore. Here are the runes scraped into
the ashtray's mouth, what is snuffed to powder
in its cauldron: its upside down dead doughboy's
helmet; its one half of a robin's egg.

Attic Order

My grandmother's centuried face
did not die with her mind,
but it remained breathing,
the face of the noblewoman

of Tyre, the eyelids folded
over in discernment.
Then she would not open
her mouth anymore, not even

to eat, not even as I carried
her beautiful things to the attic,
her pillbox hat, the silver stole,
the tight-lipped little fox, the

clamshell purse she clutched
at round tables, the noisemaker
that never touched her lips.
There was an attic order

in the columns
of boxes and the dusty light
that twisted before the window fan.
I put away the hatpin and it punished

me again, solidly pierced me
at the touch. I put away the shoes
in shut-up boxes, many powdered
tissues in their mouths.

Hymn

We are somewhere in a story,
a certain hymn begins.
It is the night the lights have failed.
My mother reclines on the couch.
The candlesticks encircle her.
My father hunches over the fuse box.
We are somewhere in a story,
the hymn goes on. It is the story
in which each of us is making up a story
and we search for each other:
we hold the candles forward
but only light up our own faces.
We are somewhere in a story,
the hymn repeats. It is the last verse
no one ever seems to know. It is the one
we mouth the words to, watching other
mouths mouth words, in the dark
church of memory.

A Blue Dish

Without my father, my mother lives alone
the first six months. She keeps things as they are.
The absences are still high up: top three inches
of the bedroom door threshold; fog of an unshined
transom; the coffee tone of dusk in porticos.

When she is gone, absence will sink down
and even fill the square blue dish
at the center of the kitchen table. It is the blue
of my father's anchor tattoo, faded to a powder;
the color of a needle's bruise below the crepe.

The dish was passed down from my father's line.
It came to this house, tattooed on its architecture.
She lives alone with it. Then the dish is mine,
its absences like apple, pear, blue color of a fall
with Icarus, soft night, little cutout stars.

In Steel

One friend, a policeman,
found a child's thumb
in the ruins of the towers.

On a bag of evidence
he wrote THUMB. "I moved
like a mechanical hand

through time," he told me,
and he went on, "just moved
one action to the next."

My friend is a good man
with a gray, punctured face.
His body was poured

from concrete. "There was
a jaw, a shattered mandible,"
and he went on,

"there was a bolt
of someone's skin, the fabric
unraveling from the arm."

My Town

Sometimes my town is deserted. The streets are dark except for a luminous bookstore window. Inside is a poet I loved in my early days. Sometimes she's talking to a younger version of herself, and they're sipping wine in unison. Sometimes I'm lost in my town, and it's raining, and I can only speak Czech.

Sometimes I'm at my mansion on the outskirts. There's a soccer field, the sun is setting over it. My guests have bled out onto the lawns. Sometimes my parents are coming down the grand staircase still dressed in their coats for winter. Hello, my father says. Hello, my mother says, in much the same way.

Sometimes I'm walking toward my town, along a giant wall, and below the wall is a river, and across the river is another place, a city of the dead, and it reminds me of the Tuileries. I know I have a choice to go there or keep walking to my town, which I always do, which I have done so far, with its spires and bars, its windows with motionless skeleton faces.

A Pair of Glasses

I find them in the sheath
of hard leather, I take
them out. In the absences

surrounding the bent-up
wire frames, the outline
of my childhood's face:

the ears too big, off
center. Eyes exhorting.
Small slope of the nose.

So little really changed
in all these years. Me
not wanting my glasses,

and the glasses, too,
I think they wanted
to be left alone, to have

their continuous tantrum;
cross-armed Bartleby,
preferring not to serve.

A Lost Cup

You drank from the lost
green teacup
in this dream:

I am the door, you said,
of the sheepfold, the cup raised
halfway to your mouth.

Your breath rippled
over the brimming, hot tea.
I think of the sheep,

crowded into their pen,
asleep on their feet,
but one of them is baying.

It struggles loose,
and I feel the sudden lightness
of an absence: like the lightness

of the hand
in which you held the lost cup,
considering its heft.

A Sunfish

At our reservoir the Pleistocene
comes alive in sudden agony
of stumpknockers, of pumpkinseeds,
of the beautiful long-eareds.
A hook in the eye is the petrified tear.

On land it flaps with its three anal spines,
coughing up air through a girdle.
The sunfish knows
that death comes from the side,
and sometimes it sees and it bites

down hard. It swallows anyway.
Sometimes the worm protrudes, a bloated
tongue. I have seen the underworld
whence it comes: black grass
that's standing up on end.

A Box of Screws

We must become someone who seeks and finds God in all things and at all times, in all places, in all company, and in all ways.

MEISTER ECKHART

Left over from some work
he tried to do, the box lay
in my father's desk, its screws
a mismatched set. Dead
in Charon's boat, the screws
bear witness to no story,
holding nothing and not
being held in their darkness
of disuse. We gave my father
paperwork to die. He couldn't
sign: the body he now hated
was his life, by God; he wouldn't
simply give the thing away.
So we left him with the pen
in hand, held strangely in his
grip like a screwdriver.

In Gold

I began to love some Elena Maria
and I thought I would die of her life.
From the window of my bedroom,
I watched as the Guadalquivir
shoved boat after boat off to sea.

From Córdoba through Seville, on to Bonanza,
and into the Gulf of Cádiz, the boats
dispersed, unhesitating: and the sun
went on setting, making everything
heavy, golden, everything deeper in worth.

There were gold horses, gold carriages, gold dung,
gold children!—dotting the Plaza de España.
I couldn't possibly afford such beauty.
As for my treasure, what else can I say.
I dragged the curtains over it.

A Doll's Head

From the screw of its neck I twist
the head, whose doll's eyes open,
slowly close. What is the purpose
of the waking up?
What was the physics of its sleep?

Nothing but tissues for brains.
The convolutions, folds and hard
creases, are a ball of smashed-up thoughts.
The tissues that were cried upon had dried
by the time I lost it years ago.

I found it in the chicken house.
Many atrocities were committed here
to which this head bore witness.
No doubt about that. Therefore I take it out back
to the small wooden block.

Glad to Be Unhappy

Today her song is Frank Sinatra's
green, melodic "Glad to Be Unhappy,"
soundtrack of this room and its good movies,
this flower spinning following light on the table
by her bed, this vigilance in wee hours.

Even in starvation, the skin pulled back
like a mask against my mother's eyes,
she is Loretta Young in *The Bishop's Wife*,
where the angel played by Cary Grant
buys her her hat. Then they skate on a lake to music.

I move like a skater, I ask her to come.
But my mother wants to stay, her masked
eyes wondering about my life. The song
is over. We are glad to be unhappy, the singer
exhorts. We are unhappy, and so glad.

The Church inside the Church Where Weil First Knelt to Pray

The church inside the church
was built at the base of the city of churches, a town
by the railway station.
You might think you are not walking inside
a metaphor; you might forget that a small yellow insect
                                  is not an allegory
that has landed on your book.

*

In the Hermitage there are caves
               each the size
of the church built inside the cathedral at the bottom
of the mountain. Simone, every part of the anatomy
has some corresponding other part,
even the ball of the knee and its heaviness on marble, high
into low, and low on high.

*

I am ready for a change, I said,
               after all this preparation.

The change for the worse will do, God answered.

I only barely stepped inside.
               And I stayed very briefly,
I bought a vial of oil
from a beggar and he wrapped it in a handkerchief he pulled,
with some prestige, out of the folds of his coat.

In Marble

The trees with their bad manners
tick at the windows of my room,
asking me to come with them,
and I remember the dining room clock
to which my father kept the key.

Face to face with the clock
and its floating black hands, he wound
it up one night. My mother set a glass
of milk on the table. The clock stood
unflinching like an admonished child.

As in a magic ritual for which
I was no initiate, the clock
began to tick. It was my mother's birthday.
The milk as still as marble. My father sat down
at his place, very quietly.

A Poetry Shop in Heraklion

It has a gabby dwarf who takes in visitors.
I have been told he'll sit and talk for hours
with his customers over the bread and the wine.

I know these shelves of authors and their books;
addle-brained boys; the serious, agitated women;
all burning themselves with bad ideas like cigarettes.

I know the way a poem pushes back the cloud
between them and their kingdom of small gods:
the wine, the olive dish, the hardening bread.

But I always arrive at the moment of closing.
I stand there knocking at the end of the blind alley,
my fist like the head of a long-extinct animal.

A Stick Figure

The man who murdered himself
in the low-ceilinged attic,
a hundred years ago, some Patrick
in our past, haunts us with a stoop,
for he was six feet tall, the ceiling only five.

Here is his long, charcoaled mouth.
His body is stiff like a stick.
This is a jolly ghost, my suicide.
This is a badly, barely fitted world,
the armpits of his best coat tight.

He drags himself on a little, then stops.
His tightened clothes are slowing him.
Time for bed, my mother calls up.
She's bent down at the ironing board,
all well again, flattening my sleeves.

Letter from Rock Creek

for Mary Oliver

I want to ask you what that clicking sound
    is named, rising out of Rock
Creek Park, below my little room; but even you
    can't help me pin that down—so many miles

from here, where you are tucked in bed, your
    little room, your neck and chin concealed by the bark
of a burnt sienna scarf;
    so I leave it

as it is, our mood music, and I remember
    shore-days in the Provincetown house,
reading in Hopkins *Send my roots rain,*
    or anything by Keats, who was

drowned in his ceiling made of flowers,
    while this click in the background
persists, not cricket, some smallest-
    insect-on-record, small enough to be

a gnat's pilot, small like a certain quality
    you have courted in your poems, how you squint
and bend down to things, how you do not disturb
    their place, how this characteristic expands

in my mind as the objects
   themselves grow tinier: the closed hood
of the mushroom's umbrella at night,
   or the clam, an Osiris, locked in its bivalves,

which made a nice supper—how the God
   appears altered, *altared*, each time you look—even the
scrape of one wing against the other's
   leathery file, to stridulate, to make a click that carries

in mathematical waves, while this singer, untroubled
   by itself, goes on fine without an advocate, a name.

The Leatherback

It is dying, this heaviest
of turtles. So magnetized

to earth, great is its labor
to be itself being, to move

with sliding steps the
brown flippers. Now it rests

in the no-man's-land of
dry sand, having lost its way

like my father did
on his way back to bed,

when he fell and I could not
lift him. The dying are always

the heaviest, until they reach
the wave.

Van Gogh's *Olive Grove: Orange Sky*

It is Saint-Rémy, many years
before the First World War,
and the armies of Europe
have not been born. Nor has the idea
of the war: it has not reached
the land which has turned red
not by the breach of shovels,
the slit of trenches, falling shells.
Let's say the land knows nothing
of the place you bring to mind.
Let's say this is not a field near Saint-Rémy.
These pools of scarab-red are not light.
Inside the creeping opening
between each branch, only yellow
globs of what is not the fog
and what is not the morning.
It is not the nineteenth century,
not even that, says the hand that commands
these forms. This is ochre used for cave bear.
This scarab is for fire, and you are merely thinking
of yourself again, who lives not in Saint-Rémy,
but in another city.

Eating Outside

UNDER THE CAFÉ TABLE
I find a small hole. It leads to a tiny café,
itself filled with tables, small shoes
at the door, chairs best suited for a vole.

And I leave as silently as I came,
like shutting my mother's closets
for the last time. Such things grow in darkness
with no effort from my life.

*

THE BUS TO PARIS took all day, all night.
A city west of Cheb is strange to you.
In our days of faithless translation, I speak in French,
but you hear Czech, but I hear English.

Chinese, the smiling waiter who snapped
this photograph. Your arm, as if reaching for something.
Your face a blur. The arm that it commands remains like that,
between the source and destination.

*

AT THE HOSPODA
twenty years ago. The man in his blue
communist jacket, now faded pink
like one of Dali's butterflies.

He is waiting for a drink that never comes.
He's still waiting for Utopia, pink,
drunk, surrounded by statues
that are pretending to be sleeping.

Empire, Discourse

When he was old my father traveled back to Rome
though forty years had passed. With my mother now
he sipped red wine out in sun along the via
Appia, when he thought he saw me wave at him
from somewhere up ahead and turn away. It wasn't
me, I was in another city, I'd try to tell him but
for the remainder of my father's life he would insist
on this story, until I started to imagine how far I'd be
by now, that road a continuous grave, the broken-
open tombs and catacombs, the turreted Aurelian
Walls, my father always coming to the end by saying
You must have had some place to get to so I let you go.

Magic

In the padlocked trunk before they dropped him
in the river, Houdini was said to foresee
his mother's death. Stuck in his box, at the end
of a chain, he felt the death, its approach,
her worry growing smaller at the eyes as she

removed herself from herself, her body shrunken
to the size of a keyhole. I believe that grief
can travel distances like that. My mother's
cough would wake me up at night, two hundred
miles away. That was a year ago, before she

got too small. She drowned in a cloud
of bright white baby hair. She lay on the bed
as if on a board, the last I saw her, still and calm.
Then truly as if a lever were pulled, she tipped
backward, out of view.

ACKNOWLEDGMENTS

My thanks to the following journals in which earlier versions
of these poems first appeared:

Academy of American Poets Poem-a-Day: "Wave"
AGNI: "Carp"
American Poetry Review: "My Carnation," "The Liquid R,"
    "Beatification"
The American Reader: "X, & Axe"
Chattahoochee Review: "The Church inside the
    Church . . . ,""Empire, Discourse"
Copper Nickel: "Magic"
decomP: "A Sunfish," "In Gold"
Delaware Poetry Review: "A Pair of Glasses"
Innisfree Poetry Journal: "In Marble," "Night of the Death of
    Seeger"
Mississippi Review: "In Steel"
Ninth Letter: "Calling Horses"
Pilgrimage: "Glad to Be Unhappy," "A Blue Dish"
Pleiades: "Magnification," "The Sibilant"
Poetry: "Attic Order"
Poetry International: "The City of Birth," "Three Feasts: Simone
    Weil"

Public Pool: "The Crow's Progress," "Van Gogh's *Olive Grove:*
Orange Sky"

Smartish Pace: "The Brahms"

Tinderbox Poetry Journal: "The Little Stairs of Z"

War Literature & the Arts: "Ardor," "Conscription,"
"Skirmish . . . ," "The Dead on Culpeper Road," "Leaving
the War," "After Charges of Desertion . . ."

Washington Square Review: "A Doll's Head"

Zone 3: "When Walt Whitman Came to Stone General
Hospital, 1864"

The translator of the epigraph from Rilke's letter to Clara
was Joel Agee; the translator of the epigraph from Hildegard
von Bingen was Dr. Sheryl Kujawa-Holbrook.

I am grateful to the following: to the National Endowment
for the Arts; to *Poetry International*, which chose my book for the
C.P. Cavafy Poetry Prize; to *Smartish Pace*, which awarded me the
Erskine J. Poetry Prize; to the DC Commission on the Arts
and Humanities; to the Danish Council on the Arts and the
Hald Hovedgaard Estate in Viborg, Denmark; and to Father
Hal Widener, who offered a summer in his home and massive
library near Max Jacob's residence in Saint-Benoît-sur-Loire.

And with a deep bow of thanks to Daniel Slager, Annie
Harvieux, Abby Travis, and Joey McGarvey at Milkweed, as
well as to my family of teachers and close readers, including
Mary Oliver, Ilya Kaminsky, Bruce Weigl, Carolyn Forché,
Yusef Komunyakaa, Eleanor Wilner, the late Peter Roche
de Coppens, the late Jake Adam York, the late Herb Scott,

Jan Wagner, Carsten René Nielsen, Lisa Russ Spaar, Dick Wertime, Jim Barnes, Mark Irwin, Juan Morales, Laren McClung, Aaron Anstett, Colleen Morton, Jennifer Richter, Jane Hilberry, Rebecca Laroche, Linda Voris, John Weiskopf, Adam Tamashasky, Bill Varner, Judy Bowles, Denise Orenstein, Bill Olson, Kim Kolbe, Katherine Larson, Sandra Beasely, David Wojahn, Carrie Hannigan, Carlos Dews, Anna Carson Dewitt, Susan Bradley Smith, Blas Falconer, the Surrey Street Poets, Chuck Larson, Roberta Rubenstein, Dori Sless, Dave Sless, Dave Singleton, Laura Dubester, Jane Goodrich, Jim Youngerman, Dana Meals, Laura Denardis, Amy Gussack, Myra Sklarew, and the unswerving and inimitable Bobbi Whalen.

David Keplinger is the author of five volumes of poetry, most recently *The Most Natural Thing* and *The Prayers of Others*, as well as three volumes of translation. He has won the T.S. Eliot Prize, the C.P. Cavafy Poetry Prize, the Erskine J. Poetry Prize, and the Colorado Book Award, as well as two fellowships from the National Endowment for the Arts and grants from the DC, Danish, and Pennsylvania Councils on the Arts. He directs the MFA program in creative writing at American University in Washington, DC.

milkweed
editions

Founded as a nonprofit organization in 1980,
Milkweed Editions is an independent publisher.
Our mission is to identify, nurture and publish transformative
literature, and build an engaged community around it.

milkweed.org

Interior design and typesetting by adam b. bohannon

Typeset in Mrs. Eaves

Zuzana Licko designed Mrs. Eaves in 1996. It was her first attempt at a design of a traditional typeface. It was styled after Baskerville, the famous transitional serif typeface designed in 1757 by John Baskerville in Birmingham, England. Mrs. Eaves was named after Baskerville's live-in housekeeper, Sarah Eaves, whom he later married.